Contents

This is ballet!. 4

How ballet began 6

Classical ballet 8

Basic move: the arabesque 10

Changing styles 12

Skills .14

Practise, practise, practise 16

Tricky move: the big jump. 18

What to wear 20

En pointe 22

Tricky move: fish dive 24

The performance 26

Give it a go!. 28

Glossary .30

Find out more 31

Index 32

Some words are shown in bold, **like this**. You can find out what they mean by looking in the glossary.

This is ballet!

Two dancers move gracefully across the stage. The music swells and the other dancers whirl lightly around them. The audience does not make a sound.

Love to Dance

Ballet

Angela Royston

Raintree

526 337 63 7

Raintree is an imprint of Capstone Global Library Limited, a company incorporated in England and Wales having its registered office at 7 Pilgrim Street, London, EC4V 6LB – Registered company number: 6695582

www.raintreepublishers.co.uk
myorders@raintreepublishers.co.uk

Text © Capstone Global Library Limited 2013
First published in hardback in 2013
Paperback edition first published in 2014
The moral rights of the proprietor have been asserted.

All rights reserved. No part of this publication may be reproduced in any form or by any means (including photocopying or storing it in any medium by electronic means and whether or not transiently or incidentally to some other use of this publication) without the written permission of the copyright owner, except in accordance with the provisions of the Copyright, Designs and Patents Act 1988 or under the terms of a licence issued by the Copyright Licensing Agency, Saffron House, 6–10 Kirby Street, London EC1N 8TS (www.cla.co.uk). Applications for the copyright owner's written permission should be addressed to the publisher.

Edited by Nancy Dickmann, Catherine Veitch, and Abby Colich
Designed by Cynthia Della-Rovere
Picture research by Elizabeth Alexander
Production by Alison Parsons
Originated by Capstone Global Library Ltd
Printed and bound in China by CTPS

ISBN 978 1 406 24946 0 (hardback)
16 15 14 13 12
10 9 8 7 6 5 4 3 2 1

ISBN 978 1 406 24951 4 (paperback)
17 16 15 14 13
10 9 8 7 6 5 4 3 2 1

British Library Cataloguing in Publication Data
Royston, Angela,
Ballet. -- (Love to dance)
792.8-dc23
A full catalogue record for this book is available from the British Library.

Acknowledgements
We would like to thank the following for permission to reproduce photographs: Alamy pp. 9 (© Pictorial Press Ltd), 13 (© Lebrecht Music and Arts Photo Library), 14 (© Patrick Baldwin), 16 (© Bubbles Photolibrary), 18 (© Patrick Baldwin), 29 (© van hilversum); Corbis pp. 7 (© Paul Cunningham), 24 (© John Bryson/Sygma), 26 (© Robbie Jack); Getty Images pp. 6 (APIC), 8 (Ian Gavan), 15 (Gjon Mili/Time Life Pictures), 19 (Gjon Mili/Time Life Pictures), 27 (Ian Gavan); Rex Features pp. 12, 25 (Alastair Muir); Shutterstock pp. title page (© Dmitry Yashkin), 4-5 (© Jack.Q), 10 (© Igor Bulgarin), 11 (© Jack.Q), 20, 21 (© s74), 23 (© Dmitry Yashkin); SuperStock pp. 17 (© Image Source), 22 (© Fancy Collection), 28 (© Flirt).

Design features reproduced with permission of Shutterstock (© AZ, © Christopher Elwell, © Arkady Mazor, © Studio DMM Photography, Designs & Art, © Plus69, © Studio DMM Photography, Designs & Art, © Robert Young).

Cover photograph of English National Ballet's production of *Swan Lake* reproduced with permission of Corbis (© Paul Cunningham).

We would like to thank Annie Beserra for her invaluable help in the preparation of this book.

Every effort has been made to contact copyright holders of material reproduced in this book. Any omissions will be rectified in subsequent printings if notice is given to the publisher.

All the Internet addresses (URLs) given in this book were valid at the time of going to press. However, due to the dynamic nature of the Internet, some addresses may have changed, or sites may have changed or ceased to exist since publication. While the author and publisher regret any inconvenience this may cause readers, no responsibility for any such changes can be accepted by either the author or the publisher.

Why I dance

Saskia Beskow, a dancer with the New York City Ballet, says, "It is natural for me to move to music. It makes me so happy to dance."

How ballet began

Ballet was popular in the royal palaces in Italy and France. King Louis the fourteenth of France adored ballet and loved to dance. He even danced as Apollo, the Greek god of the sun.

King Louis was known as the "Sun King".

Pantomime

Ballet dancers have always used special gestures, or movements, called **pantomime**, to help to tell the story.

Classical ballet

Many classical ballets were created in St Petersburg, in Russia, after 1850. The ballets included *The Nutcracker*, *Swan Lake*, and *The Sleeping Beauty*. These ballets told a story, like a fairy tale.

A scene from *The Nutcracker*.

Dying swan

Russian ballerina Anna Pavlova is most famous for dancing "The Dying Swan". When Pavlova was dying she asked to hold her swan costume.

Basic move: the arabesque

An **arabesque** is a common position in ballet. The dancer stands tall and stretches out one leg behind. The arms are stretched out gracefully.

The move is called *arabesque en l'air* when the leg behind is lifted.

Here the male partner supports the female in an *arabesque en l'air*.

French terms

The first ballet school began in Paris in 1669. Today, most ballet steps and positions still have French names.

11

Changing styles

About 100 years ago, ballet companies in Paris, New York, and London began to dance new, shorter ballets. The dancing was more important than the story in these new ballets.

Spectacular sight

Sometimes famous artistic people like Pablo Picasso and Coco Chanel made the sets and the costumes.

Skills

Ballet dancers must be athletic, or fit, as well as elegant. They need to be flexible and have strong muscles to perform different moves.

George Balanchine

Choreographer

A **choreographer** creates all the steps in a ballet. George Balanchine is a famous choreographer. He started New York City Ballet. Balanchine created more than 400 ballets in his lifetime.

Practise, practise, practise

Professional dancers practise every day. First they warm up at the barre, which is a long wooden pole fixed along a wall. They might do *pliés*. They stand tall with their legs turned out and bend their knees over their toes.

barre

Dancers follow the actions of their teacher.

The ballet dancers then move away from the barre. They move on to centre work. They practise jumps, turns, and balances.

Tricky move: the big jump

Grand jeté means "big jump". It is a **dynamic** way to cross the stage. The dancer does the splits as he or she jumps through the air, with arms stretched out.

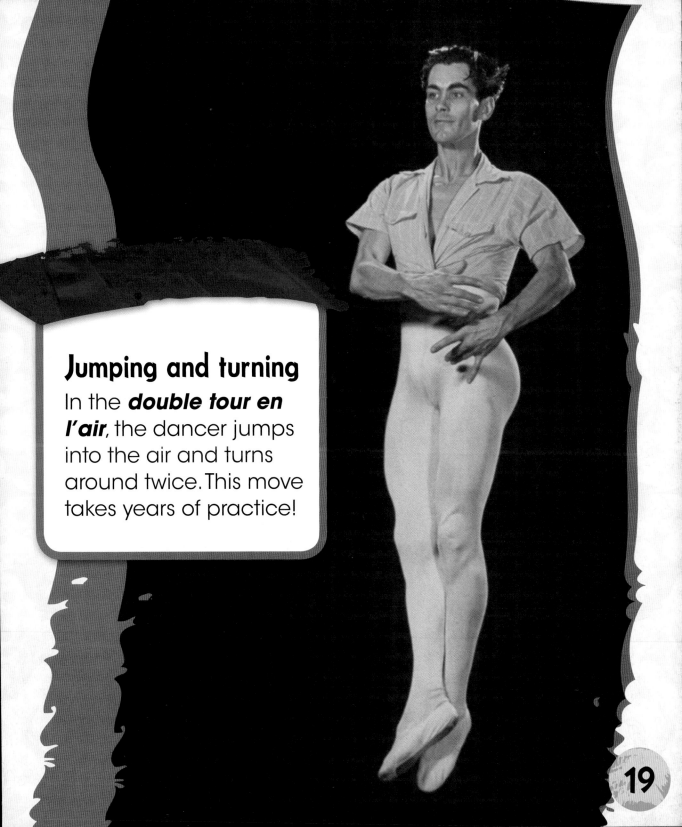

Jumping and turning

In the **double tour en l'air**, the dancer jumps into the air and turns around twice. This move takes years of practice!

What to wear

Most dancers wear a leotard when they practise. Leotards are comfortable and stretch as they move. Dancers perform in specially designed costumes. In a classical ballet, the ballerinas usually wear tutus.

tutu

Ballet shoes

Ballet shoes are the most important part of a dancer's clothes. They are soft to allow their feet to arch and stretch.

En pointe

Professional ballerinas often dance on the tips of their toes. This is called **en pointe**. Ballerinas wear special *pointe* shoes that support their feet. The shoes have hard ends and flat toes.

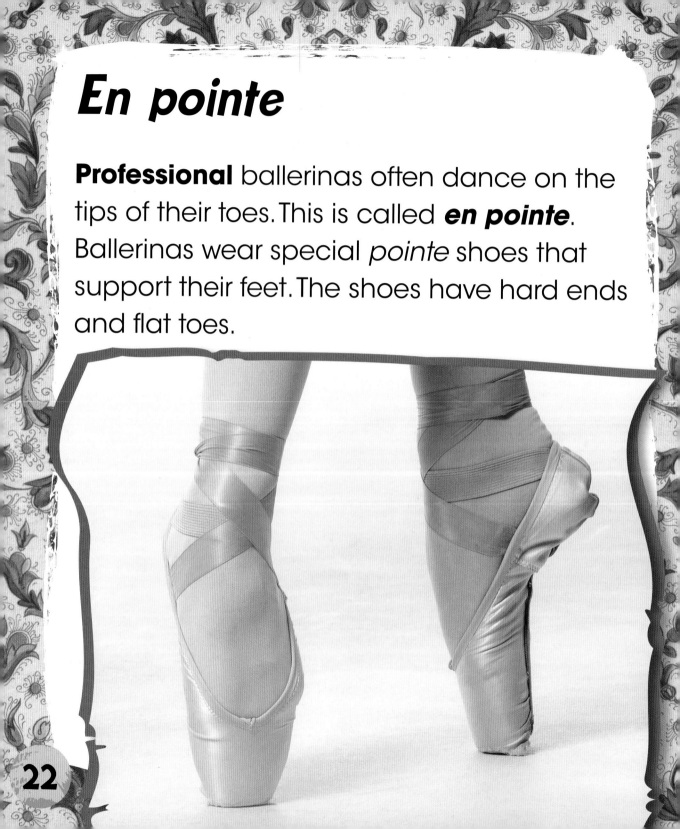

Be patient!

Your ballet teacher will advise you when you are ready to go *en pointe*. If you start too young it can hurt your feet.

Tricky move: fish dive

A **pas de deux** means "a step for two" in French. It is a dance for two dancers, usually a man and a woman. It uses jumps and lifts. It sometimes ends with a spectacular fish dive.

Rudolf Nureyev and Margot Fonteyn

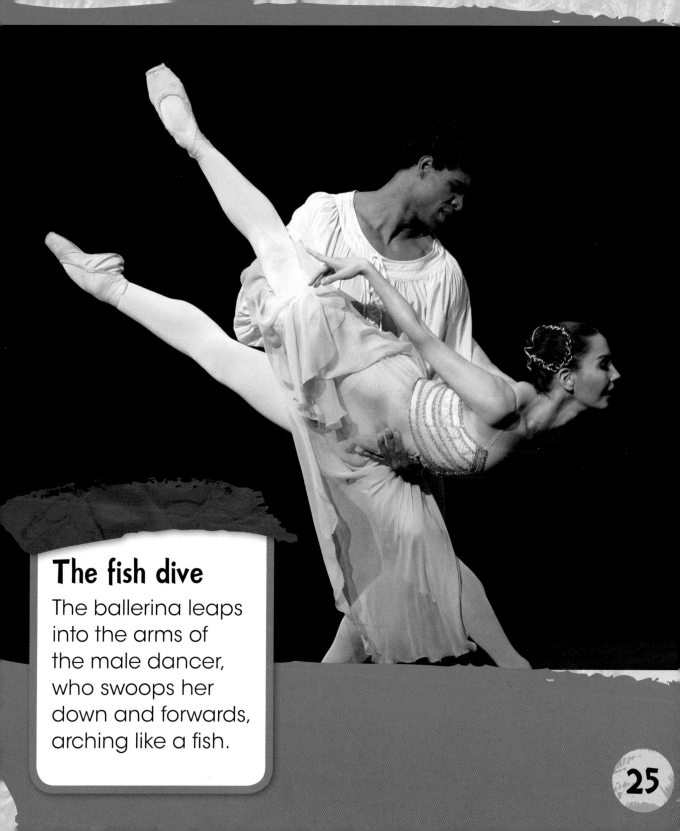

The fish dive

The ballerina leaps into the arms of the male dancer, who swoops her down and forwards, arching like a fish.

The performance

You can watch ballet on television and on DVDs. But the most exciting way to see it is in the theatre. A large number of people are needed to put on a ballet.

The Nutcracker

Behind stage

Set designers and costume designers work for months to make the sets and costumes. The dancers practise and rehearse lots of times.

Give it a go!

Ballet is a lot of fun and great exercise, but you should learn it with a trained teacher. Ballet makes your body stronger and it helps you to balance. Joining a class is also a good way to make new friends.

Getting confident

Ballet makes you more confident about your body. When you are ready, you can perform for your family and friends.

Glossary

arabesque position with one leg stretched behind and one or both arms reaching forwards

choreographer person who creates and designs the steps of a dance

double tour en l'air French for "a double turn in the air". It is a jump in which the dancer turns twice in the air.

dynamic describes something that is energetic and exciting

en pointe French for "on point". When a ballerina balances and dances on the tips of her toes.

grand jeté French for "big jump". A jump in which the dancer does the splits in mid-air.

pantomime way of telling a story or showing thoughts and feelings using hand or head movements

pas de deux French for "step for two". A dance for two people.

plié French for "bend". A movement where the dancer bends their knees over their toes, and then stretches their legs straight again.

professional person who is paid for doing a job

set designer person who decides what the stage in a ballet will look like. This includes objects, for example trees or tables, and painted background panels showing a scene.

Find out more

Books

Ballet (Get Going: Hobbies), Lisa Dillman
  (Heinemann Library, 2006)

Ballet Dance (Snap Books), Karen M. Graves
  (Capstone Press, 2008)

Mad About Ballet, Lisa Regan (Ladybird, 2011)

The Ballet Book, Darcey Bussell (Dorling Kindersley, 2006)

Websites

www.ballet.org.uk
This is the website of the English National Ballet.

www.roh.org.uk/discover/ballet/index.aspx
This is the website of the Royal Opera House in London,
which includes the stories of famous ballets.

www.scottishballet.co.uk
This website includes photos, videos of performances, and
interviews.

Index

arabesque en l'air 10, 11
arabesques 10–11, 30

Balanchine, George 15
barre 16, 17

choreographers 15, 30
classes 28
classical ballet 8, 20
confidence 29
costumes 13, 20, 27

designers 27, 30
double tour en l'air 19, 30

en pointe 22, 23, 30

fish dive 24, 25
Fonteyn, Margot 24

grand jeté 18, 30

history of ballet 6–9, 11, 12

leotards 20
Louis, King (Sun King) 6

Nureyev, Rudolf 24
Nutcracker, The 8, 26

pantomime 7, 30
pas de deux 24, 30
Pavlova, Anna 9
Picasso, Pablo 13
pliés 16, 30
practising 16–17, 27

sets 13, 27, 30
shoes 21, 22
skills 14–15
Sleeping Beauty, The 8
Swan Lake 8, 9

teachers 17, 23, 28
tutus 20